TRANSITIONAL MAN

TRANSITIONAL MAN

the anatomy of a miracle

FRANKLIN EARNEST III
M.D., Ph.D.

Far West Editions
San Francisco, CA

Library of Congress Catalogue Number: 81-68047

International Standard Book Number: 0-914480-06-5

81 82 83 84 85   10 9 8 7 6 5 4 3 2 1

To my teachers
To my family
To Transitional Man

CONTENTS

INTRODUCTION

I am grateful to Dr. Frank Earnest for this little book, which bears gracefully such a substantial message.

As the subtitle indicates, it envisions the extraordinary changes in the human brain's electrical circuitry which may flow from a rightly directed work of self-study.

According to Dr. Earnest, a principal cause of the present worldwide fall toward crisis is that the scientific study of the brain, as well as its functioning, has been confined to the physical or biological level and increasingly locked into the goal of physical well-being and survival. The role of the brain at higher levels—in the vast realm of metaphysics—has been neglected. The possibility that the brain can play a part in the process of changing itself is barely noticed, even though it may be the unique responsibility of man, by virtue of this change, to fill a place between the worlds upon worlds above him and the animal, physical world below.

Now that the whole human experiment is felt to be in danger, it is obvious that we have overreacted to the extraordinary physical facts about our nature that modern science has revealed. Other possibilities of mind function are being spoken of today. Many people, for example, are becoming aware of the effect that ideas have on the quality of their lives.

The way back is not easy. Only a few will resist the requirements of the social order, which is almost everywhere under the sway of Western science. Science can never make physical measurements of metaphysical energy transformations. But the hope exists that, with the necessary help, a small number will verify, step by step, the ladder of adjustments and changes in man's being that finally permit his brain to function in an orderly way on higher as well as lower planes.

This is Frank Earnest's concept of *Transitional Man*. "The recipe for any understanding of life—physical or metaphysical—is essentially the same," he says. "Persistent motion in the direction of the goal is required." Since true knowledge is related to the whole being, not just to one or other part of it, indirect learning by which one part, the mental apparatus, teaches the others will not help. Metaphysical knowledge is direct, immediate.

As he hands us the keys of a method, Frank Earnest demands no jumping off cliffs or holding of hands in a circle. All the necessary changes begin from the cultivation of self-awareness, leading to recognition of the different forces and movements of energy in man and his environment, and their possible relationship with each other through the formation of new structures within him.

Medical science, even though its goals are so limited, has in the last century adventured boldly into the unknown and brought back immeasurable benefits to mankind. American medical disciplines are admired throughout the world. With a distinguished career as a neurosurgeon behind him, Frank Earnest brings to his subject first-hand information on all that contemporary science knows about the brain, besides the clear, unruffled thought that we expect from a doctor.

But it takes more than even the best medical training to open us to the return movement towards higher levels of brain function and neurophysical integration. The knowledge and motives developed at the level of ordinary life, even in the present atmosphere of imminent planetary crisis, can never be enough to show the way back beyond a certain point. Ideas and knowledge of the whole cosmic order, coming down from a level where Truth is One, are necessary, together with guidance in relating them to the physical level. This further training, certainly no less demanding than the first, Frank Earnest was fortunate to receive from Olgivanna Lloyd Wright, one of Gurdjieff's earliest students.

Does Frank Earnest bring out sufficiently clearly what an arduous undertaking is this work of self-transformation, how seriously it needs to be taken? In any case, to give due warning of the dangers and difficulties of the Way without making people afraid to use their imagination creatively is a delicate matter in which all who assume the task of transmitting great ideas take the measure of their own understanding.

First publication of this book by Vantage Press was in 1978. I appreciate the generous attitude with which Frank Earnest accepted our offer to discuss and revise the original text with him, particularly Chapter VI.

JOHN PENTLAND

ACKNOWLEDGMENT

A man is a composite of all his springs, his winters, of all his happenings, of all his wishes. His creation belongs to everyone he has met and to everything he has experienced in all his lifetimes. From the influence of the casual glance of a stranger to the meaningful guidance from those who love him, there are countless other contributions that ultimately serve to awaken him to his own reality. Still, in the face of this, there lingers the need to mention a few who to the author have been a source of special magic.

I am thankful first for my parents who provided a home permeated with fundamental concepts of Christian ideas which became significant to me later on, and who encouraged me in the pursuit of my desire to be a neurosurgeon.

Olgivanna Lloyd Wright was my teacher through the very tedious times of my spiritual beginnings. It was she who called my attention to the sounds of a higher consciousness through the teachings of Gurdjieff. The Christian principles first described to me by my parents and by two Sunday School teachers of long ago (A. B. Campbell and M. B. Townsend) were given life. Through the tribulations of this birthing, new meaning and understanding of life became possible.

John Pentland, one of the original students of Ouspensky and later of Gurdjieff, will forever have my gratitude for finding *Transitional Man* interesting enough to warrant his concentrated effort to examine and improve the delivery of the message of this book, and in continuing the endless work process through dialogues with me about man and his possibility.

I am grateful also to Jacob Needleman, Professor of Philosophy, San Francisco State University, for his careful examination of the text and thoughtful suggestions.

There are others whose response to the text helped to improve its expression, but acknowledgements would be incomplete without recognizing the forbearance of my family who witnessed the resolution of this human experiment and the devotion and patience of my wife, Alice, who watched, encouraged, and supported this effort to produce *Transitional Man*.

TRANSITIONAL MAN

CHAPTER I

MAN IN PERSPECTIVE

Wfind himself in a dilemma of such consequence that his
next step could seal his own destiny? We can begin a search
for realistic answers to this question by first looking at him in
perspective—as a significant event in the history of a universe,
as a human experiment in progress.

No matter what religious, philosophical, or scientific disciplines we subscribe to regarding man, in some way they all
seem to tell us that 'the earth' was prepared for his appearance.

If we choose to read Genesis, we will find a recitation of
creative events that brings man into the scene at the end of a
series of cataclysmic days during which the firmament was organized, vegetation appeared, and animal life came to the sea,
the air and the land. Then man was created in God's image
to rule the lower kingdoms, and to subdue the earth, and pop-
ulate it.

If we examine the scientist's revelations, we will find a strik-
ingly similar tale of beginnings. Man is described as the endpoint of legions of purifying battles, mutations, inventions,
blind experiments, successes and failures in the course of his

ascendency in the biological pyramid from the anlage of a single cell. Reminiscent of this climb, man relives *in utero* the drama of this creative sequence with each conception beginning as a single cell and passing quickly through the metamorphological progression of the animal kingdom to the birth of man.

No one really knows what steps may have been taken in the creative act that led to man's appearance. It should not disturb us or subtract from the marvel of creation to suppose that the human form came into being either as a result of a succession of orderly creative events or as a single miracle. The significant fact is that man is here, and the earth and its contents are submissive to his whims.

A deeper examination of the changes we see in the progression of the animal kingdom, both phylogenetically and embryologically, reveals that most of the action has centered around the development of the nervous system, culminating with the blossoming of the cerebral hemispheres in the human brain.

Simultaneously, there is noted in this history of change a steady improvement in the adaptability skills of the host as the animal kingdom prepares for a sudden leap into a new dimension of perception and understanding with man's arrival. We are given hints of the ultimate significance of the brain as it increases in size rather suddenly and becomes more and more protected, resting finally in a lake of fluid, locked in a bony sanctuary called the skull.

To facilitate the completion of the brain's task in its planned cyclic course through the atmosphere of planet Earth in a span of time called life, it comes equipped with a space suit of skin, five categories of sensors for the assessment of the environment, arms and legs that give it mobility and special skills, reproductive organs to insure continuity, and life support systems to provide for local viability. During its sojourn, the brain can direct its equipment in terms of both its physical strategy in behalf of local adaptation and its metaphysical strategy in behalf of behavioral goals.

Accepting man's presence under these circumstances, we can then scan the march of events through the jungle warfare of trial and error that characterizes the struggles of the animal kingdom and observe the trends in the implementation of these strategies.

We notice first there has been a trend toward greater versatility in the theme of adaptation and with man we see him tower with unquestioned preeminence high above lower forms as a genetic witness to all that has happened in the selection between what is adverse and what is beneficial to the organism.

Throughout this theme there is evidence from behavior that within the most basic cellular form there is instilled with creation a propelling primordial plan—an inherent creative thrust, a deep protoplasmic wish, an *a priori* demand—which programs the terms of existence on this planet. Locked in every creation there is the necessary updated information which we call instinct that insists on two actions for earthbound participation—survival and procreation. However, the possible transactions permitted by each form are very limited and could be described as a very tight circle of activity with little happening within the species for millions of years until we come to man, when there is sudden unusual flexibility. When the circle was too tight, whole units were wiped out (e.g. dinosaurs), but with the advent of man, for the first time in the animal kingdom, the activity found permission to escape the confinement of survival and procreation demands. Through the addition of new circuitry to the brain's organization, man became equipped to break the circle of instinctive requirements and foster new ideas. In addition to the ancient theme of 'local adaptation', there arose a new theme of creation calling for total adaptation as a part of a higher metaphysical goal—an ultimate sense of perfect blending and harmony with the universe.

But the new theme requires yielding allegiance to the old theme and man resists this change. At the same time he stands poised ready to take a gigantic step in a new behavioral direction; he drags with him the modified yet persistent extrapolation of primitive instinct which holds him tenaciously to its survival and procreation theme so long as he has protoplasm to protect and to produce. Since man's instinct represents the cumulative concentrate of survival knowledge—a genetic memory—he holds to its historical importance, and as a consequence would appear to remain almost inexorably attached to the automatic, biochemical, basic behavioral programming of a single-celled animal, both as a witness and a performer, as though he were overpowered by its ancient ritual. Instinct persists, seemingly limiting man's role to that of the 'preserver' of the human experiment.

We can see the limitations of man's metaphysical strategy directed toward new hypothetical goals by taking notice of his behavior in today's world. One need not be a psychologist or a behaviorist to notice that we are in the midst of an era of social paradoxes, extreme rights and lefts, radical group expression, forceful group action, and warlike violence, if not open war. Searching the wide horizon of human behavioral activity and restlessness which extends roughly from the swamps and jungles of Vietnam to the rather sophisticated theme of satellites, rockets, and atomic physics, we can readily see that most of man's responses can be reduced to physical strategy—to an animalistic formula that lays quick claim to violence or the threat of violence for most of its transactions. In this scene of eat and be eaten, man becomes the most ferocious expression of the survival demand. Like all animals he will kill in behalf of survival drives, but unlike most animals he will kill his own kind singly (murder) or in large numbers (war) to suit his survival purpose.

In the days of the caveman, as the brain activated the hand with increasing force and purpose, this meant quick, decisive, and final confrontations, but in our age the same impulse has come to set in motion a kind of calculating dialogue and cunning deployment of lethal skills, which, however, lead ultimately to the same social disaster.

Within a relatively short time from Neanderthal man up to the present era, the convolutions of the cerebral hemispheres have folded themselves into billions of new circuits but they still remain hooked to instinct. So far, they seem to have served only to allow man to refashion his clubs of yesterday into devices of such proportion that at present, if destiny should meet him with some unresolvable moment, his brain could once more activate his hand to push the button that could destroy his whole world.

Certainly this has become an overreaction to the wish to survive. It is an abusive expression of cerebral function. It cannot be that this was the reason for the development of so intricate an instrument as the human brain. All animals have engaged successfully in survival and procreation contests with less equipment. Man has not yet trusted the evidence of the

5

special significance of his own form by which he might escape from the tight circle of a single-celled animal to the exciting goal of universal harmony. He has not yet accepted the forecast of behavioral change which his own brain signals.

The cyclic pattern of civilizations found in any history book still places man in the Darwinian survival contest but now with one disastrous difference. By virtue of the genius of his creative skills misappropriated in behalf of survival folly, his rise and fall drama can for the first time end with his own total destruction. If survival of the fittest is the eugenic formula guarding the suitability for life, man, at the moment of his greatest opportunity to take the next step in behalf of his own growth and development, stands ready to declare himself unsuitable for the universe.

It is difficult to accept the idea that what has taken eons of time to produce could be interrupted by the chain of events linked to a single mistake—a single button—an atomic holocaust, a possible planetary explosion. The human experiment seems too valid for such an end. Yet, we will have to concede at this moment, as man seemingly prepares for his own annihilation, his present behavioral theme is a failure. Only the rapid expansion of his consciousness to meet Providential claims for him can deliver him from his dilemma.

We are still in the sixth day of Genesis though night is approaching rapidly. Man is in transit in the story of creation, but in transit where?

CHAPTER II

MAN CLOSE UP

FROM THIS BROAD overview of man as a significant and peculiarly special event in the history of a universe, let us watch him through a finer lens during a lifetime.

It would seem the very circumstance of his entrance into the atmosphere of planet Earth is prophetic of the foreboding setting in which his drama is to be enacted. In the midst of his quiet parasitic repose *in utero*, he is suddenly struck by violent evidence of an impending change. Rather precipitously he becomes rhythmically beaten and compressed by piston-like strokes of force until he is delivered into a totally new environment—an event so traumatic, his entry starts with a cry, a cry which in a certain sense lingers throughout his entire lifetime.

Though it is an accepted fact that man's birth is attended by travail, it is not so well understood that his life is also attended by travail. This expulsion from a former sequestered homeostasis, dramatically announced by the convulsive contractions that set him free from his maternal mooring, brings with it the first requirement for survival—he must breathe. What he does not yet know is that this is only the beginning of the requirements demanded of him to demonstrate his continued right to belong to the circle of time called life, which ends strangely enough with another paradoxical, final requirement—that he stop breathing.

In that interval set between breathing demands, he must struggle. The duration of his battle will depend upon the effectiveness with which he copes with the physical deficiencies he has inherited, the illnesses and injuries inflicted on him by his environment, and the intangible segment of time built into his protoplasm by the creative force which is kept from his discernment. Even under the most ideal circumstances, man at present must experience a physical death for his breaths are counted before he is born. To these governors of time we must add still another factor, man himself. Man is his own worst threat to life while at the same time he is the channel for his own rescue.

Now, because man is a developing form both in the overview and the short view, he does not arrive with full knowledge of how to conduct himself, especially since he has acquired a brain which does not always insist on instinct, but provides him on occasions with a choice of behavior. Some choices are learned through pain to be unwise. The initial cry of entry is probably not an accidental forecast of a general overall objection to survival problems—especially as the circle of action becomes greater, demanding more flexibility and at the same time allowing for more mystery.

Since his learning will come mainly through experience, and since he does not know exactly how to conduct himself in this strange land of many new sounds, smells, and tastes, his first sense of security—of belonging to it—begins with learning the sound of his mother's voice, the smell of her body, her touch, and particularly the taste of her food. His needs, especially for food, continue to be heralded by a cry. By filling his immediate needs 'mother' quiets him for brief periods which are filled with sleep, but gradually there is more and more wakefulness to which is added other voices, other smells, other touches, and other tastes to which are then added visionary samplings, a sense of form, then color, and finally from the assortment of sensations there is added a concept of what is satisfying and what is unsatisfying.

Most of this first knowledge is the product of a special combination of his mother's instinct and his own instinct to survive in spite of basic ignorance regarding the precise reason for things and even the reason for survival at all. With time and repetition of experiences, he begins actually to enjoy the new combinations of sensory formulations, which together become an adventure filled with surprise. Soon he will smile and replace his cry with signs and sounds of a growing adjustment.

As his exploration continues, his attention falls back on himself and very cleverly he sucks his thumbs, plays with his toes, fondles his genitals, and experiences his excreta—generally with satisfaction. Though he can see his hands and feet and other forward parts, he is denied the sight of his face and head—the protectorate of his brain. They are kept out of view and require the use of a device such as a mirror for an approximate idea of them (and even then he glances cautiously to the right and to the left stretching the perspective, hoping to see more, not ever being quite sure how he really looks throughout his lifetime). Still, he is permitted to see these physical features in others and so it is he raises his vision from his own beholdment to discover he has company on planet Earth and there are other people in space suits like his, who have hands, feet, and other body parts, except they have faces and eyes that catch his attention.

The idea that is hard to get used to is that earth's experiences from the beginning are attended with pain. The very nature of the trial and error technique requires man to suffer. There is a common denominator to all of man's real learning—suffering. But man suffers whether he learns from it or not, and the sufferings vary as the lessons of earth vary. They do not belong exclusively to the poor or to the rich, to the white or to the black, to the young or to the old, for each has its own kind of sufferings, and the summation of them during a lifetime is as essential to the ultimate expression of man's spirit as food is to his body.

Now we can define suffering at this stage as the consequence of the difference between things as we think they are and things as they really are. The degree of the disparity is the measure of the degree of the suffering. The disparity is fed by another feature that mushrooms with man—his imagination. Although man does not as yet know a better world, he can imagine one. His brain permits the formulation of answers to problems, though confined by the force of instinct initially to survival problems. His brain can conjure up the local antidote for his immediate misery. But also man's imagination fosters dreams which try to lift him from his physical plight, becoming behavioral goals for him.

Still, man cannot seem to bring what he imagines to be desirable behavioral goals into his earthbound life. Though he uses his imagination successfully to cater to the comfort of the body, he is unwilling or unsufficiently motivated to apply the same skill to the building of foundations beneath these behavioral dreams of himself. In fact, accomplishment in behalf of the cause of local physical comfort seems to subtract from even the slight urge he may have to devote attention to his eternal dimension. His preoccupations with physical earthbound matters tend to dull his sense of concern regarding his own metaphysical future. Still, the proof lies all about him in his inventions that what he imagines is possible. Man walked on the moon because he imagined it first. By the same token, if man imagines freedom, he can be free.

To watch a child discover the law of gravity gives us some idea of what needs to be done to bring imagination to practical terms. It becomes an example of what may be necessary with any lesson on planet Earth to fulfill both physical and metaphysical goals. With his first step he falls. His fall represents his ignorance of the law, his miscalculation in bringing the imaginative idea of walking to reality. With each successive fall a little more knowledge about walking is acquired. His brain, eager to perform in his behalf, remembers the physics of each event and gradually develops the formula for successful execution of the idea of walking. Soon he not only walks but runs—and more than this—his brain, now understanding the law of gravity through experience, places the performance on automatic. He no longer needs to think about it.

Just as the child falls many times before mastering the law of balance, discovering the line of harmony through a series of painful experiences; so man must learn other lessons both physical and metaphysical by suffering temporary failure until the center line of the concept he seeks is mastered. Just as in learning to walk, the brain is organized to define the most distant idea so long as man moves in the direction of it.

Every experience has unknown boundaries when first explored. To the child some voices he encounters will be too loud, some smells unpleasant, some tastes too horrible for the stomach to accept, some sights too ugly, and some surfaces too harsh to touch. At the same time there will be other experiences which are pleasing and satisfying. By a combination of what is established as best for him through instinct and what

11

accrues as best for him through experience, real knowledge is acquired—useful proven information—which is filed away for future encounters through memory. It is memory that allows for the further development and integration of consciousness.

Once the child has learned to walk the challenge changes. Where does he walk to? Aimless meandering is not satisfying —not fulfilling. He is not satisfied just to walk about his mother's skirts. His first adventure is to walk from mother to father; his exploration is confined to the familiar—to family. It is a friendly experience basically, for there is genetic camarad- erie that insures safety. But sooner or later he walks to an untried person and this becomes more difficult, for now his exploration captures the countenance of someone he has never seen before—who looks something like the familiar but has a different sound, smell, complexion, in other words is strange to him, a stranger. The familiar was comfortable like the womb was, the strange is uncomfortable because it is capable of surprise like the outside world was when that first draft of air struck his face and made him cry.

Although man soon comes to understand that every fresh encounter in the stranger circle carries an unknown factor with it, he discovers also that by design mystery inflames his curiosity, for also packed into his protoplasm as part of the creative wish is the overwhelming pledge to explore and to overcome. As man learns to walk, he moves steadily from the known toward the unknown.

So, stranger or not, his protoplasmic computer—his brain— prepared for the expansion of its tasks, allows him to venture out and approach a new target—a stranger—and all goes well until he sees to his surprise and consternation this new face with arms and legs like his is playing with a toy—his toy—a toy that shortly before gave him pleasure, a toy that a few minutes ago belonged to him, and suddenly the walk is not so satisfying, especially when he is struck in the face with his toy as he tries to reclaim it. Dealing with this matter is the beginning of a new kind of knowledge that one continues to acquire throughout his lifetime.

The first reaction to the toy dilemma elicits a behavioral response that is picked from the limited repertoire of a limited experience. Since attention was gained initially with a cry (which was a signal for an honest need—food), it is employed once again for the reacquisition of a toy. However, since the problem now does not involve survival, it attracts less attention. The response found so effective before must quickly be revised, for without the biased intervention of a third party (mother), crying accomplishes nothing.

The challenge here, and the challenge for the rest of one's life, has to do with finding ways to deal with toy matters. Of course, even at the beginning, if one is big enough, the solution may be simple—one simply takes it back—but if the issue cannot be solved by force, other techniques for claiming toys will have to be learned, especially since toys are not necessarily essential and are designed more to give us pleasure than to help us survive. One could easily argue, however, that sometimes toys bring a mixture of these benefits. There are some who would say all toys and all experiences are in a certain sense essential. "We get what we need and we need what we get." We shall see.

In any case, most of man's activity from this point on in his ordinary development consists of battles over toys. Only the size and character of the toys change. A teddy bear becomes a car, a boat, a plane, a home, a country, a planet, or people—especially certain people—in which case all other toys become

13

expendable in the cause of seduction. The bigger the toys, in earthbound terms, the more skills are necessary to collect them. This leads us to a consideration of man's 'Essence' and his 'Personality'.

CHAPTER III

MAN IN COSTUME

IN ADDITION TO INSTINCT, which is a packaged genetic memory representing the hard-earned lessons of the animal kingdom, birth also brings a fresh formula for each individual creation, representing the roulette-like matching of chromosomes at the time of conception.

We will not complicate the problem at the moment by seriously introducing considerations of why certain pairings take place except to say they may not be as accidental as they seem, for in fact they may be preordered on the basis of universal needs, species needs, and individual needs (karma). Rather, at this time we will simply say that children of the same parents are different, not only in sex but in hereditary traits. Though we can see physical resemblances in progeny, we must concede each is unique not only in form but in performance, and it is this uniqueness that gives us individuality. No matter what this identifying formula dictating special behavioral patterns consists of, we can for the time agree to speak of it as the Essence of the individual.

Usually the behavioral features characterizing Essence can be associated for ease of observation with certain animal characteristics. Some individuals for instance will have the basic nature of a deer. They are sensitive, fearful, and their game plan in a world of violence is to run and hide. Others, by sharp contrast, may behave like a bull, performing with quite an opposite pattern. They are aggressive, fearless, and continuously ready for attack, challenging rather than running. Between these wide extremes are many other behavioral formulas which when observed closely depict certain features of other mammals. But even within these animal groupings, there remains individual specificity. It is the Essence of the individual that is unique and identifies each creation.

To begin with, Essence makes its needs known within the 'family circle', and except for minor sibling skirmishes these needs are usually easily met. However, the same techniques that were workable at home are found to be unworkable in the 'stranger circle', especially when dealing with toys. One cannot simply take a toy from a stranger without evoking a reaction which now is out of the reach of parental control.

Since this is a common problem among individuals, especially among groups of strangers, patterns are established in the herd for meeting these issues. Basically, the accepted technique in the social order for dealing with toy matters requires that one win, earn, or deserve the toy on the basis of rules for bargaining.

For instance, one could buy the toy, but then to buy the toy one needs money—man's present measure of value—and to earn money, one must perform something. Ideally, one must be able to do something that has value, not just for oneself, but for someone else as well. One needs to know something special. To know something special one needs to be taught by someone who already has acquired purchasing power in the marketplace. One needs a teacher, so schools are formed, and in a certain sense we could call education training for toy business. If one wants to buy only little toys, one need not be taught very much, but if one wants big toys, one must be taught very much. In addition to knowledge one must acquire something in order to have success at the marketplace. One must develop something very special; one must develop Personality.

Personality is the costume fashioned to cover up Essence and, actually, we hide within our Personality. Sometimes we speak of it as our image, the picture of ourselves we wish others to see. We need Personality because Essence alone fails in complicated toy transactions in the stranger circle because it is too direct. It operates directly in terms of its individual needs as dictated not only by instinct but also by its own requirements for growth determined by the defects and aspirations coupled to the specific genetic formula of the individual. It usually has no diplomacy, salesmanship, bargaining methods, or leverage mechanisms to satisfy either its needs or its desires. Essence remains close to earth and sinks its fingers into the soil for the answers to its questions; it does not understand why this basic operation is not adequate at all times.

Actually, the closer one remains to earth, the less need there is for Personality as the toy demand there is low. Consequently there is less need to acquire either knowledge or Personality for there are few major toy transactions.

Certain occupations (farming, forestry, fishing, etc.) attract people who are inclined to live in their Essence, close to nature, close to their animal world, as they were born. They have relatively few toy needs. Characteristically they are honest, direct, uncomplicated and content with the earth. Their contact with Personality is minimal. They approach the marketplace with suspicion, a suspicion born of a sharpened instinct because they are close to earth, rather than a suspicion

17

born of sad experiences in toy deals. They are wary of Personality natively, for they sense through the roots of their survival knowledge that it is contrived, even deceitful. They enjoy a simple childlike excitement over little toys that did not cost very much but which also did not require them to costume up in order to obtain them.

At first this sounds ideal, for since there are fewer toy demands, there are fewer problems. But also, there is less chance for change for the excursion in life is limited; there is less motion, less exploration, less adventure, and consequently less opportunity for growth in knowledge and understanding. Personality is necessary for success at the marketplace and the marketplace, where Personalities gather, is necessary for the development of the individual. At the marketplace we have a better chance to see ourselves. It becomes the mirror by which we eventually become able to see our own faces and to discover our own nature. Problems arising from the intensity of toy business provide us with the experiences essential to our most meaningful revelations of life.

We must remind ourselves that man comes equipped to move about and respond to the inquisitive nature that arrives with him. He is endowed with a most intricate, boundless, and miraculous computer—his own brain—which was created to give him access to the secrets of the universe; but problems —sufferings—are essential if he is to move with an idea to its core. With each lesson in pursuit of the challenge, the line of harmony becomes more sharply defined and his understanding doubles, triples, and compounds itself to a new level of consciousness.

Toys, for the most part in those early years, are things— usually shiny, glittering, colorful, dynamic things that move,

spin, or feel good. But sooner or later, toys become people—
especially the shiny, glittering, colorful, dynamic ones who
also feel good. This alteration in toy composition and this shift
in the form of toy interests arrive with the modification of
earthbound programming from mere survival to include the
second basic requirement for eligibility as a passenger on this
spaceship. In accordance with the dictates of his ancient protoplasm—his animal heritage—man must not only survive, he
must reproduce. Rather suddenly one day, to remind him of
his built-in obligation, the sex force pours into his tissues,
revising his body contour, changing his voice, and taking over
as the motivating drive behind his every action. From here on,
the toy game has to do with seduction. The phallus becomes
the axis about which his world spins.

Because nature has rehearsed its acts so many times and
has staged and restaged its survival and reproductive performance so often, the timing of this new surge of power is
almost synchronous with the structuring of Personality. It
appears just as the wardrobe is being fashioned and a special
costume is designed called 'charm'. Charm is simply Personality preparing to rape under socially acceptable terms.

Now Personality is the contrived exterior of man—the false
self insisted upon by the social order for all arrangements
between people who want toys, especially big beautiful toys,
now sex toys. Armies have been deployed in behalf of the
harem and behind every battle can be traced a thread of continuity which leads, sometimes ever so subtly, to the fulfillment of man's most exquisite bodily pleasure, the ultimate
physical sensation—orgasm. This convulsion of pleasure of
such an incomparable order, connected by the wisdom of the
creative force to the dictum to reproduce, places man in con-
tinuous pursuit of its attainment. Even if he resents being

prisoner of this impulse and tries to deny its significance through either oaths of celibacy or permissive indulgence, it still haunts him as long as he lives. In truth, most of the motivation in his everyday performance centers on enticing a prize into the bedroom. The yacht, the plane, the bank account, the suave manner called charm all work together to manipulate his sex object into bed.

The social order, recognizing the seriousness of this new force that steers man's actions, rushes to the situation to fashion appropriate arrangements to deal with this overwhelming and disruptive addition to the instinctive survival demand of life on planet Earth. Because of the appearance of this sudden surge of unmanageable power, unleashed as a response to the requirement to reproduce, the herd constructs rules of behavior formulated essentially around a contract for love called marriage. To insure lasting tranquillity in this bond built initially by biological blending, vows are spoken declaring this heavenly happening will last for a lifetime. But sometimes the biological part fades, the Essence breaks through the costume of charm, and what was thought to be heaven becomes hell. Somewhat reluctantly, and usually at great expense both physically and metaphysically, the social order allows for the reclaiming of vows through still other rules spoken of as annulment or divorce, leaving one free then to subscribe to different vows subsequently for another heavenly happening. The community becomes very confused later, especially when the children of these happenings look for their parents' guidance.

Man also backs up his system of order by organizing his sense of God—his reverence and subconscious respect for the creative force he watches. He tries desperately to capture his spontaneous, boundless thoughts of the infinite in a finite framework worship called religion. Relentlessly, he tries to squeeze his inspirations into a comfortable ritual he can refer to and recite, forgetting that if his thoughts have no freedom to move, they cannot grow. Because there are so many organized ideas about God, men begin to be separated into groups and sometimes there is terrible war between religions that differ about the language of God's message of love. Loyalties to the messenger begin to exceed loyalties to the message, while worship inappropriately drifts from God to his prophet. Under such circumstances the universality of the theme of love as the common denominator of man's ultimate goal is soon forgotten.

Together, tradition and dogma become the guardians of ordinary man's social order. He needs them because he has not yet come to realize that if he were in harmony with his true destiny he would not need them so much. When man's consciousness is raised to a level where he can understand what love is, he will already be in some degree of harmony with the universe and its laws.

Through the deployment of his Personality, man tries to improve the circumstance under which the acts of survival and procreation are to be conducted. He gives style to violence and rape under the sponsorship of the social order as he modulates them to wealth, prestige, power, and courtship. Man in costume becomes the negotiator at the marketplace.

No matter what the motivation, Personality allows a man to move about in the herd, blend with it, and transact whatever toy business he has under acceptable terms so long as he stays within the framework of rules and ritual. One then performs his acts, meets his real and false needs through Personality negotiations, and at the same time hides his Essence—his real nature. What transpires then in the social order is that business is not transacted between people (real people) but between Personalities and even between multiple Personalities within the same individual, for one costume may be found suitable for one occasion but unsuitable for the next. With acquired accomplishment at the marketplace, a man can learn to choose the costume that is most likely to gain the toy he wishes in any given situation. Eventually, experiences in the stranger circle (the marketplace) become a succession of costume parties. At the ball, we may see clowns, kings, queens, devils, angels, doctors, lawyers, priests, educators, scientists, etc., according to the costume; but actually devils may be dressed like angels, or as we say, wolves may be wearing sheep's clothing. Actually, the ballroom, the marketplace, may be filled with thieves and murderers depending on how badly toys are needed.

If the costume is assembled properly, one can approach a stranger who holds a desirable toy and begin negotiations using a rehearsed technique—perhaps slapping him on the back in conjunction with a fine compliment followed quickly by a statement of good faith—and, depending upon the personality skills of each individual in the confrontation, some change in toy status is likely. Friendships so established for this brief transaction are called acquaintances and are seldom durable for they are intended to last only until the toy transaction is completed. The whole performance is contrived, each individual hoping for a slight edge in the exchange. In every toy transaction there is *double entendre* with the true motive hidden. Yet, it is the adopted social way for toy bargaining, for it is thought to induce calm and eliminate violence. Actually, since the goals are usually vicarious extensions of the survival theme, it does neither.

When Personality is the 'winner' in successful toy transactions, it comes to be thought of as the supplier of our needs,
both real and false, and soon one begins to identify himself as
the Personality and inadvertently begins to believe his own
act. For instance, one day, preparing for toy business, a man
says to himself, "Today I will play king," but in the course of
the transaction, especially a successful transaction, he may
begin to say to himself, "I am king." Since he is not a king,
this ends his chance for real development, for now he has
completely lost sight of the fact he is hiding.

Because toy transactions in the social order are conducted
through pretense negotiations, the distribution of the toys
becomes unjust. Bargaining based on survival intrigue is not
always fair. The law of compensation, activated with creation
which measures all energy allocations on a precise scale of
cause and effect, is abandoned in the marketplace. Through
bribery, favoritism, thievery, murder, and a false value scale of
performance, toys are passed frequently to the undeserving—
usually the most powerful, the most wealthy, the most organized, or the most cunning. This defect in the distribution pro-
ceedings may rest with the individual or, more than likely,
may involve clusters of individuals called corporations who
choose to bind their talents and resources together and act as
one person at the marketplace because certain groupings add
power to the bargaining position. When the distribution eventually becomes too lopsided, unrest develops in the herd.
Gradually the injustices reach such an unbearable level that
some frustrated individual triggers a rebellious reaction that
then spreads wildly through the angered mob. Murder ex-
pands to war as waves of social pressures meet to redistribute
toys. But the new order, being prisoner to the same impulse
to acquire, carries with it the same blemishes, and the market-

place is essentially rebuilt as it was, because man remains like he was.

The undulating pattern of civilizations attests to this repetitious sequence as the law of compensation swings back and forth over the objectionable scene repeatedly, wiping it out. The unavoidable consequence of falsity and its by-product injustice is disaster. What man does not seem to comprehend is that he cannot own anything, anyway, that is marked with earth's trappings. Even his breath belongs to earth and he must give it up. Toys are loaned, and they are loaned for a purpose.

Personality, set free of purpose, develops its own appetite. With avarice it moves through the marketplace, sweeping as much as possible into its pockets, becoming pompous and vain as its accumulations grow. Its demands mushroom while the growth needs of Essence are forgotten. Soon, because of his unusual acquisitions, a man gathers his toys together for his acquaintances to marvel at and be envious of. He invites others to see his collection and by their acclaim he can satisfy himself that both he and his toys are truly unusual; for since he has smothered Essence, he has lost his real sense of their true worth, and the recognition of their valuelessness to him as a mere collection.

Repeatedly, the Personality world gathers in groups for mutual reinforcement of toy goals. With forced festivity submerged in the chemistry of alcohol or drugs, the false documentary becomes easier to bear. When the noise quiets down, the assembly quickly regathers again for Personality cannot bear the benefits of silence.

CHAPTER IV

ORDINARY MECHANICAL MAN

ORDINARY MECHANICAL MAN is the man we have been describing so far. He is a man who has lost sight of himself and of his potential. He has pledged himself to the perpetuation of falsity, though unconsciously. He is motivated by fear—fear of his outcome in toy matters and fear subconsciously of his own disclosure not only to others but even to himself as well. He fears his act will be discovered—his Personality act. His goals remain survival oriented—wealth, prestige and power—which he mistakes for security. His reproductive goal, frequently the inadvertent by-product of his seduction activities, is children. It pleases him to see his own image and gives him another sense of power as he takes credit for something out of his control. In a sense he is fulfilling a primitive manifestation of the wish to be eternal. He does not think beyond earthbound limits. He sets to rest any higher needs by mechanically reciting ritual. The unknown and the unseen are uncomfortable to him and he delegates the translation of such matters to scientists and priests who report to him in agreed upon terms of comfort. He abdicates his responsibility to question—to even question himself. His every act is self-centered—selfish. He pretends he knows what is best for him when at his feet are the ashes of his decisions. He pretends he is in control while he continually bursts through his frail network of rules with unspeakable violence to weave a pattern of universal misconduct.

Because of the circle of survival and reproductive interests in which he performs his repetitious acts, they become automatic. His responses become mechanical. He becomes a creature of habit. He submits to conformity, the preamble of social calm. He is ordinary because his vision is limited to the ordinary, confined to the local, circumspect matters of a brief physical life. He has not yet caught sight of the special role intended for him on planet Earth.

Ordinary mechanical man, because he remains a prisoner of his earthbound drives, is subject to three basic laws—the law of Providence which is responsible for his creation; the law of nature (cosmological law) which describes his place in the pattern of cyclic events in the universe (astrology, I Ching, etc.); and the law of accident, which weaves an unpredictable path through the human experiment.

So long as man remains an ordinary mechanical man, he is subject to the combined influence of these laws and his schedule of events is uncertain and out of his control. Only if he senses his potential and his true role as a transitional form can his planetary course be clearly established. Only then can he escape the confinement of cosmological programming and the intrusion of accident. Only then is his contact with Providential law unencumbered.

In spite of ordinary mechanical man's failure to sense his mission both from a personal and a planetary viewpoint, so long as he breathes, the opportunity exists for his possible emancipation from the prison of his animal drives. Always there is the outside chance he will escape his chains and do what he must do—suffer the pain of seeing himself as he is, asleep to his real purpose.

If we examine his performance in more detail, we will see that by virtue of his organic nature, his Essence, he reacts to a stimulus preponderantly in one of three ways—with his body, his mind, or his emotions (feelings). Usually he reacts with a combination of all three; yet still, in each individual, there is sufficient dominance and regularity in the choice of reaction to describe him as Physical, Intellectual, or Emotional. Even though there is great overlap—because we are all mixtures —there is sufficient similarity to notice there is a behavioral pattern in each category.

Once the performance pattern is established simply by each type falling into its habitual natural trends, revealed through noticing the repetition in technique in toy negotiations, we can virtually forecast the format of the future decisions and actions of that individual so long as he remains an ordinary mechanical man. In other words his behavioral program is locked in.

Physical man, for instance, believes that nearly all matters can be dealt with physically. Frequently his physiognomy will attest to his game plan. He tends to be muscular—even over-muscular—and remains forever anxious to demonstrate his feats of strength. The theme is acquisition by force. "If you want a toy, take it." By this formula, if deployed without restraint in the herd, toys accrue to the strongest.

With primal man this was a quick and final encounter as violence filled both survival and harem needs. Conquest and seduction were not so subtle. Even now there remain echoes of the reverberations of those early one-to-one encounters as they linger in certain competitive sports (body contact sports) where strength is tested in controlled confrontations. The excitement of this physical drama can fill any stadium with spectators to watch a form of man's beginnings in toy negotiations.

The basic transaction requires few costumes and essentially it could be described as the 'tough guy', which always contains a modicum of bluff. At the moment of bargaining one can fight or run depending on the situation, but the repertoire of responses is somewhat limited by the nature of the theme.

Though the physical type may adhere to physical dimensions in his performance, he may spread his activity sufficiently to take advantage of some of the accomplishments of the Intellectual type; and the transaction pattern in toy matters thereby becomes modified, though still a physical theme— still on the edge of violence. This alteration is not then due to a change in his basic program, but rather is probably a result of what he has borrowed to improve the effectiveness of his physical response to the toy challenge.

We will see later, as we study intellectual man, that he enjoys thinking and gathering information which, when applied to problems, can lead to inventions and improvements in dealing with survival matters. He may not implement these discoveries personally, but they are readily grabbed up by physical man to reinforce the principle that the strongest deserves the most.

Usually these revelations of intellectual man lead to substitutes for muscle which are helpful to physical man, especially a weak physical man; and so a spear is fashioned, space comes to separate the contestants over the toy in question, and the outcome is not quite so certain, though still the result of violence. Victory no longer belongs to those with the most muscle, but possibly to those with the most spears. The word strength is modulated to weaponry. Gradually, a bow and arrow places the contestants still farther apart, and with the appearance of gunpowder, great distances separate them. Soon muscle has less and less to do with the outcome.

Finally, still borrowing from intellectual man, he comes to the uncanny position of being so powerful in weaponry he needs only enough muscle to push the remote control button that could not only destroy the contestant but could destroy his whole world and all of its toys. With this fact, we have exhausted the usefulness of violence, the negotiating theme of the physical type, for we have carried the transaction to the point where it becomes clear that on a physical basis alone there is no future.

The intellectual type finds another method altogether for the acquisition of toys. His emphasis is on the mind and his theme is thinking. He becomes the official intellectual witness of his environment. He notices there are rhythms in life and cyclic patterns that are orderly and have predictable schedules. He knows, for instance, that the stars are disposed each night in a certain pattern by which he can mark time. He knows that sunlight and rain make seeds become plants, that plants can bear berries and become food, and that if he cultivates the land he can plan on certain crops. He learns to trap herds of animals which he then domesticates and butchers as the need for food arises. He finds that his energy is more expeditiously used if he lays claim to a certain space and lives there, where he can homestead and reproduce in more comfort.

What he discovers mainly is that by thinking things through, even with the most fundamental improvements in

29

survival skills, there is time left over. In other words, he has acquired leisure. Now what happens to leisure can spell the destiny of both individuals and civilizations. Leisure that is filled with idleness is deadly. Leisure that is filled with work is also deadly, if it is the wrong work—work born of the wrong motive, work limited to earthbound matters only.

In the case of ordinary mechanical man, in this case intellectual man, leisure gives him still more opportunity to observe and assemble more facts. As the gathering of information continues, there accrues more knowledge than one man can deal with expertly by himself; thinking interests begin to fall into categories and specialization results. Facts about stars he calls astronomy; facts about the structure of things he calls engineering; facts dealing with health he calls medicine; etc. With time, communication improves to the point where exchange of data becomes almost instantaneous and major discoveries are quickly filed away in computer libraries. Those with a mastery of facts are called teachers, and information tends to be localized in universities where both teachers and libraries are found. As more and more people learn facts, the toy market becomes a very complicated business.

Ordinary mechanical man, now the intellectual type, finds that facts are negotiable in the matter of toy transactions and to become educated is ultimately to place one's self at an advantage in the marketplace. The more one knows, the greater advantage he has for one simple reason—he can influence other people in the realm of ideas. He can cause others to behave in certain ways to his advantage—he can manipulate them. Knowledge becomes power—not power to subdue through violence directly, but power to seed thought, to convince, to argue in favor of, and hence ultimately to manipulate man's actions in one's own favor. In the meantime, he can induce physical man to fight his battles for him. We say he has become cunning.

Since one is rewarded to some degree by the number of facts acquired, information is translated into cash. As money has toy acquisition capabilities, it cannot be kept just anywhere; because physical man, realizing its value, will resort to his own technique for toy matters and steal it—take it by force. To prevent this, intellectual man has large, heavily guarded buildings constructed called banks, where he can put his money and hide it so that no one really knows how much toy power he has. Later then, at his discretion, he can buy a toy he has been wanting.

Since great numbers of people are educated and banking money and since there is violence close by at all times, the intellectuals, who are gathering more and more rewards for their facts, hire physical type men to patrol their streets or march about in large groups called armies to prevent any inadvertent loss of toy purchasing potential.

Of course, as it turns out, all ideas that intellectual man gathers together, which he in turn uses to convince and to argue with, are not always received with uniform favor and it may require exceptional cleverness to disperse them successfully. Just as there are muscle struggles, there are idea struggles, and sometimes the ideas are completely opposite to each other and cause great threats to the banks.

If the problem involves very large groups, such as countries, those hired to protect the monetary system of bartering for toys, that is the street patrols and the armies, are asked in the interest of security to subdue those with opposing ideas. So intellectual man, fearing he may lose the money with which he can buy toys, figures out ways to equip his army with more and more destructive weapons. He rushes from his laboratory continually with fresh information about the organization of the universe—the macrocosm and the microcosm—funneling each fact into a formula for destruction until finally he finds through great perseverance he has unlocked the secret of the cohesive force of the universe which he can reduce to a simple formula—$E=mc^2$.

With these three letters, known by intellectuals, intellectual man stands ready to erase his enemy with one final explosion. But the price of this is his own world, and very suddenly we have reduced his position to precisely that of the physical type whom he now employs—namely the position of total violence and no future.

Now to be emotional about toys is probably the most tedious and least understood technique of bargaining in the case of ordinary mechanical man. In the emotional type, as we might expect, emotion pours out with sudden explosive quanta of energy that stun the body and confuse the mind as it belatedly tries to figure out just what happened in the toy transaction event. However, if we examine the emotional spectrum that ranges from grief to ecstasy or from hate to love, we can see very quickly it is the world of feeling as far as ordinary mechanical man is concerned that has been the most neglected. In fact, the herd is so frightened by its unpredictable dynamics and potential power, it has taught from the beginning, with the first cry over toys, that it is wrong to cry—that it is best to hide emotions. "Don't let your contestant know how you feel" is the standard advice. So an attempt is made to rule out the emotional type from the start by fencing emotion in and smothering it.

But emotional expression, especially in the emotional type, cannot be held in check by mental devices. In spite of social censorship, the display of various emotions in toy acquisition projects can become a technique for bartering.

Going back to that first toy confrontation in the stranger circle, the child's first reaction, borrowed from survival needs, was to cry. But to regain a toy, the same cry that was useful for food requirements was no longer useful in the stranger circle. Still, emotional man found he could use a modification of this reaction form by creating a disturbance of a kind reminiscent of the cry. He could still sound a behavioral objection. The cry of disappointment could be modified to pouting, punishment by withdrawal, refusing to participate in the toy transaction, or at least pretending not to participate. The cry, changed to pouting, could then move on to anger with even stronger evidence of disappointment, spilling then into temper tantrums with physical overtones such as throwing things, stamping, running away, etc. Frequently in toy business this led to an early return of the toy to stop the disturbance and in a sense the emotional type was rewarded for the trouble he had caused with the very toy he wished for. In the social order this is called: being spoiled.

In other cases, when the outcome of a toy transaction seems too uncertain, the emotional type could call upon sympathy as a technique for reacquisition. He could 'cop out' by developing a headache, or some hysterically based physiological defect that excused him from the unpleasant, cumbersome, and uncertain negotiations. If he were skillful enough, the herd through social sanction, misdirected guilt, and contrived remedies would send its representative to his very door with the 'needed toy' properly packaged and tagged with a message of sympathy.

These emotional techniques of a rather primitive order are not the only ones available to the emotional type. He may discover, for instance, that to register great happiness can be useful. He can become ecstatic about receiving toys so that it becomes a happy experience for someone to give him a toy. In a sense he is saying, "I will smile for you if you will reward me."

Up to now these emotional methods for toy bargaining are fairly benign though they are not useful for true growth and development. A more malignant and very dangerous form of emotional expression comes with the extreme of disappointment when anger turns into bad temper, then into hate, for hate is always destructive. Hate immediately wishes to harm its adversary—the one holding the toy.

What we must take notice of with emotional reactions is that they are characterized by lightning-like changes in form. They do not follow the same time scale as the mind which draws out the problem, reasons, and tends to evaluate information in order to come to a so-called logical conclusion. And the body, when compared to the speed of emotional change, is practically at a standstill. Physical changes are so slow our eyes can perceive them. By comparison, emotional reactions are virtually instantaneous.

Since anger can change to hate in a flash and since hate always wants to destroy without even consulting the mind, it can commandeer the physical form to act in a violent way—bypassing the mind. Hatred can grow and spread quickly because it is contagious. The mood of an individual filled with hate can spread to a mob filled with hate like the spread of a fire. It can rather quickly involve whole segments of the herd —even countries. Whole countries can then come to hate other countries and use all of the accumulated skills of intellectual man to destroy the adversary, the object of hatred, and with this sequence we are once more back to the same endpoint—at the brink of total destruction with no toys and no future.

It would seem that ordinary mechanical man, regardless of his type, insists on trying to reduce his world to a physical unit. All his information—even if it was imaginative at one point—is forced eventually into a sensory definition. He says he must have proof—tangible proof—if he is to maintain the purity of his observations of the existence of things. He stretches his senses to their limit, adding inventions and contrivances to extend his fingers, but always he carries his data to the laboratory where he insists there must remain some kind of ash in the crucible if the findings are valid. If there is no ash, there is no validity. Only what he can see, feel, smell, taste or hear fits into his program. He may speak of unseen things with agonizing reservations—he may even pay homage to higher abstract ideas through mechanical philanthropy—but at the same time he does not choose or even wish to spoil his comfortable formula for truth by bringing them into his life or by having them influence his preset concepts.

Courage, for instance, is an abstraction he is content to think of in association with combat or its more sophisticated modification, competition. He is almost unmindful of the courage it takes to suffer a disappointment silently. A tear is annoying water on the cheek to him. It does not seem important to notice how much sadness might be crowded into just one of them that falls inadvertently. All of this is too abstract, too impractical, too unproductive, too weak—and yet ordinary mechanical man must learn to cry if he is to grow.

CHAPTER V

MAN AWAKENED

THE MOST SINGULAR physical manifestation that declares man has been prepared for a unique task on planet Earth is the human brain itself. As the nervous system developed, we watched it appear as a bud and then virtually burst into a full bloom with the arrival of man. The cerebral hemispheres suddenly expanded and became the heralds of a new potential consciousness; the dawn of new behavioral possibilities. Man found he was equipped not only to change to meet the demands of environment with exceptional capacity for adjustment, he could also cause environment to meet his demands on a limited basis. He could change dark to light, cold to warm; and through his inventiveness, he could move swiftly through the sea, the air and over the land. He found also he could even escape the planet for brief periods. Still, the most exciting capacity of his brain he has barely noticed; yet it is the high point of creation. Man can change himself. Through the proper use of his brain, man is capable of overriding instinct and altering Essence. Man is the first of the animal kingdom to be offered a choice of responses. Ordinary mechanical man has within his reach the ability to lift himself out of the circle of mundane survival-reproductive animal programming. The human brain has become the command post of a totally new human experience. There would be no need for its complexity if the activities assigned to it were to be confined to the circumspect matter of survival and reproduction alone. The whole animal kingdom has been capable of this with far less equipment. The human brain symbolically tells us that man is ready to cast off his animal bondage. Within the folds of the cerebral hemispheres is the circuitry for escape.

From the simple fact that the brain is structured and functions as an electrical instrument, it is reasonable to suppose that the thing that plays upon it, namely consciousness, is also electrical in nature. Tucked into the folds and crevices of this mysterious organ are billions upon billions of electrical schemes whose circuitry still remains immune to our most updated scientific evaluation. Though the skull could not long hold back man's exploring fingers from its depths, the disclosures only declare that the brain's organization is of such a high order that we can rightfully expect surprise in behavioral performance.

Responses need no longer be simply moving toward or away from a stimulus based on purely survival or reproductive interests. Although the electrical circuit tends to follow old historically based pathways and to reduce response to the simple and expedient act on behalf of instinct (the lazy route), the possibility now exists that as fresh information is channeled to the brain through its end organs, it can be processed, refined and redefined through multiple augmentary and inhibitory relay systems to yield an innovative response. With his brain man has the opportunity to assimilate a wide spectrum of stimuli, to move about and gather distant samplings of his environment, to mix old with new through memory, to contemplate, and finally to add imagination to the electrical recipe.

37

The result can be a new response to an old stimulus. The end product of this electrical machination is creativity.

But man need not limit his observations of the human brain to its physical dimensions. The brain is far too delicate to permit the revelation of its secrets by the use of lesser tools. Man must expand his assay of the human brain to include its metaphysical dimensions as well. He must be willing to step across the boundary established arbitrarily by science in its sensory examination and roam unshamefully in the realm of ideas, in the world of the unseen, and let the human brain demonstrate without restriction just what it is capable of. Although science has given us a peek at the brain and placed us in awe of its complexity, we must come to see that the only laboratory capable of revealing the intact brain's possibilities is the individual himself. Each of us has the validity of his own experience. We are the proof. Man becomes the living testimony of what he discovers.

We could watch an animal for thousands of years and because of its repetitious pattern we could just as well call it a robot. But man need not be a robot. Even if science's laboratory can yield no proof of the human brain's metaphysical implications by its standards, the individual's own evaluation of the human brain, by the very circumstance of the study, can establish the magic of its function. By accepting new ground rules defined through personal experience, he can use his own brain, directing its energy as he sees fit, as a method of describing its significance. He thereby becomes the witness and the verification of its miraculous performance.

Man cannot escape the opportunity within his own laboratory which his own life provides to verify that what he imagines to be possible is possible. The elimination of the experiment by a stout scientific declaration of denial of the terms of experimentation because they deal with the abstract, in no way eliminates the experimenter, the experiment or the laboratory—man himself. Statements of distrust of the unseen, no matter how officially they are issued, cannot discount the significance of the unseen, and the brain's ability to deal with the unseen, to the experimenter who is locked to the experiment by birth. He might as well deny life itself. The individual who pursues an idea cannot escape the full implication of it in his own life because of his own living. The idea will rub off on him in spite of his declared allegiances. It continually breaks out of whatever sensory formula he attempts to impose on it and affects him.

Man's consciousness calls upon the human brain to translate its distant messages into earthbound language—body, mind and emotional language. Man's actions are a rendition of his level of consciousness.

Smothered beneath the fumes of old violence, the noise of survival, and the grinding teeth of man's perverted appetites, there is audible to him an inner voice that raises behavioral questions, challenges his right to destroy his world and himself, and calls for a new level of consciousness. New ideas, foreign to his ancient protoplasm, hover over him, and though they are strange to him, they are somehow acceptable because of the long preparation of his unique brain to receive them.

As man's destiny on his present course becomes more critical, the inner voice becomes more perceptible. It calls to him from every spoke of his wheel; he must change. The ecologist, the physicist, the economist, the priest, the farmer, the philosopher, and the metaphysician all cry crisis.

Man cannot continue to run in his present circle of destruction unabated, unmoved by his own information. He must see that at his present level of performance he only accelerates his own demise as he overpopulates his world, robs it of its resources, exhausts its energy, and pollutes the land, the sea, and the air with the debris of his own selfishness. Man must awaken and listen to these new sounds counter to the perverted survival drive. Give! Share! Sacrifice! Love!—all challenging instinctive rights. They call for complete abandonment of violence at the marketplace.

This inner message, hopefully touching the consciousness of ordinary mechanical man, leads eventually to the formulation of a question within him—a question that produces the birth pangs of a new man—a possible Transitional Man. The question that reaches him in some form is—Who Am I?

This question, asked in so many variations (Why am I here? What am I doing this for? What's it all about? Where do I go from here?) can become the beginning of man's break with the animal kingdom. If he listens more carefully he will hear the theme of a whole new behavioral world—man must love, he must love God and his neighbor as himself. But who is Self? The task is given to him in reverse order. Before he can love anything he must know who Self is. He must sense the significance of his presence here.

To the social community, which is still geared at present to the local programs of survival and procreation and its perverted extensions, questions of personal identity arising in a man's consciousness represent a threat to the stability of the social order which tries always to establish conformity, insure a forced calm, and oversee all toy games. Questions of this type are not useful to these goals, for with the discovery of the answer, the questioner may no longer fit quietly into the pattern established as best for him in the herd. With the answer, the questioner could become an individual and individuals by definition cannot be counted upon to perform blindly in the tight circle. A true individual's behavior can no longer be predicted by the herd in toy transactions. He cannot be programmed to conform or to not conform for he tends to resist the mechanical acts which fill the marketplace. His responses are spontaneous and are subject to alteration in tempo with his own growing concept of truth.

Society's first reaction to this frightening phenomenon is to make more rules, hoping to discourage signs of initiative and fatigue the innovator with paperwork. This sequence compounded leads to the production of more rules than any one person can master because now many of them are in direct conflict with each other. Because of the questionable meaning of each phrase a whole profession develops around rules pretending to produce justice, exploiting the confusion for personal gain while making a noisy, futile attempt to provide man with an interpretation of just how he is behaving rulewise.

If a man continues to be troubled by the unanswered question, other measures can be summoned up to nudge him back into his mechanical role. The rehabilitation can begin by offering him more education to improve his lot in toy games. The enticement of better rewards can sometimes distract the questioner from the question. If successful, he will become diverted from his inner turmoil as he pursues "how to make a better living in the marketplace" rather than "how to make a better life on planet Earth."

If his inner torment increases in spite of various supportive systems, the psychiatrist may be called upon. Generally, because of the unfortunate economic circumstance of this confrontation, both the therapist and the patient are forced into a prefabricated plan of social goals, designed to return the patient to society as he was—a functioning unit—rather than to proceed on the adventure of returning the patient to himself—a project that would need to be innovative, demanding of both the psychiatrist and the patient, costly, time consuming, and uncertain (maybe unsuccessful). The psychiatrist is handicapped not only by the sheer numbers of patients who stand at his door waiting upon his palliation, but also by the fact he himself may be a prisoner of the same social malady. Frequently, as a matter of logistics, if nothing else, the patient is offered a chemical solution to the problem—a tranquilizer—which may be temporarily helpful at the time of the dishevelment, but which can hardly be expected to disclose the meaning of life. Rather it tends to dilute the question until hopefully it disappears.

These efforts, designed to maintain the status quo of the social order, may provide temporary stability in human interplay about toys but they only put off what must occur in the human experiment. Man must eventually answer the question—Who Am I?—if he is to find meaning in his life.

For the individual, there is no more important moment in the unfolding of his consciousness, nor one that is more critical for his fruition than the moment of this question. With this sudden arousal of personal awareness, man stands peculiarly alone, surrounded by unfriendly forces, the armies of tradition, dogma, family, social hypnotism, the frailties of his own Essence, and lingering instinctive drives; all of which beg for the overworn circuitry of history—the easy, expedient, ready answer—'acquiesce and conform'. If he decides to become 'the seeker' looking for the answer to the question (Who Am I?), ready to accept the reality of its disclosures, he must also be ready to suffer the grief of being unique in the human scene. If he falls back into the social formula geared to struggles for comfort, power, wealth, prestige, and all the false goals of Personality, he will fall also into the rut of animal bondage which he mistakes for security because in its depths he can no longer see over its walls. His consciousness and his brain no longer serve their real purpose. He disappears into the mirage of the social sea of superficial orderliness which remains quiet because it is asleep.

If he decides to pursue the question, he will launch upon a search that will lead him out of the labyrinth of tradition and dogma and all the impediments set as traps for him by the social order as he climbs the mountain of himself to a higher viewpoint. He pays homage to his physical world because his feet are there, but his head is directed toward a distant goal—harmony with his God, his neighbor and himself. His cerebral skills will permit him with perseverance and a strong wish—a deep prayer and an unprecedented will—to express the fresh spontaneity of freedom as he constructs a new scale of values, values he was created to understand.

It is this man we have spoken of as ordinary mechanical man who can awaken to this special responsibility to become the bridge between the animal world beneath him and the spiritual world above him—each claiming him. If he awakens to his identity, he is caught in the struggle between these two worlds for he is in transit from one to the other. The destiny of the man of our fantasy depends on the outcome of the struggles of this man who awakens and begins to move toward his new behavioral goal—a man we could call *Transitional Man*. Such a man is awake but unfinished.

CHAPTER VI

TRANSITIONAL MAN

IN THE PRECEDING chapters we have made some observations about man. We have seen him as the Creator's special manifestation on earth—at least at this moment. Man is clearly the current culmination of the creative impulse, regardless of his history. As such, he is endowed with an instrument of consciousness—the human brain—a phenomenon of such high order we cannot as yet fully appraise its uniqueness. The complexity of it resists our finest methods of investigation and even our most exciting revelations of its potential provide only hints of its possible ultimate capabilities.

We have watched man appear on earth in the overview and in the short view, and we have seen him fulfill his survival and reproductive requirements characteristic of all animal life on this sphere. We have watched him cover his Essence with Personality as he goes to the marketplace in the matter of toy business. There we saw him fall into the rut of repetitious performance, a performance that revealed his own failure to see his true role on earth—a bridge between animal bondage and spiritual fulfillment. We observed him become virtually an automaton, a creature of habit, an ordinary mechanical man, forsaking his exceptional attributes while he abused his own world.

We have also noticed his perplexity when a certain question arose in his consciousness at some point in his development (Who Am I?)—a question which could have become the key to bringing new meaning to his life if he pursued it.

When this question is taken up more seriously and the dynamics of its puzzling implications begin to echo throughout his tissues, man can set in motion a whole new dimension of living. If he truly seeks for the answers, he experiences a kind of awakening. He becomes what I have called a Transitional Man—a man on the way to completion, a man who is changing.

Much work is required in the interval between the asking of the question and responding to it fully—not just in thought but in deed as well. The search must begin first with the wish to hear the answer in depth. A man engaged in such a search must be sufficiently sensitive to the arousal of a deeper current within himself by the question, that the wish to seek the answer is simultaneously generated. If the wish is not imbedded in his consciousness, he will have difficulty launching into the pursuit of the answer, an action incorporated in the question itself. Unfortunately, no one can give him that wish.

But the wish only accounts for the commencement of the search. To proceed not only with enthusiasm but with endurance, one must develop or redirect another force within him— a force called Will. For the man who has been successful at the marketplace, it is more than likely he has already tapped into this force in behalf of survival interests and their extensions of wealth, prestige, and power.

We said earlier that survival success depended not only on the skills of instinct but also on the flexibility of the skills. With the advent of man we saw instinct reach its most flexible opportunity in the implementation of survival and reproductive demands, but we also saw the chores of instinct spread into the circuitry of the cerebral hemispheres and commandeer this higher organization to perform on its behalf. The result was the production of ingenious destructive devices of such purport that the whole human enterprise came into jeopardy. The space suit and the appendages of man, designed for the brain's convenience, became the masters of the very creation they were intended to serve. The brain became the slave of the body and succumbed to its demands for comfort and pleasure.

But even in this subverted role, the brain makes its mark and compels us to marvel at its capabilities when its facility is directed through man's focused desire toward a specific goal. Nothing seems impossible for it even in response to the wrong cause. We watched its circuitry respond to man's demands to conquer the land, the sea, the air, and outer space as he donned yet another space suit, escaping earth's tug for brief periods of interplanetary exploration. Man is a determined creature. He has proven over and over again that when his brain is touched by an idea in a certain way—no matter how imaginative the stimulus may seem to be—he can accomplish the mission the idea arouses by applying a certain kind of attention to the task. This attention polarizes his energy in behalf of his goal, channeling his Will, which then promotes the processing of the electrical charge through the brain's elaborate structural network where earthbound symbols are formulated. Here the idea becomes translated in the form of action into the physical manifestation the idea sponsors. Through dedication to a specific aim, man develops a new intensity of consciousness by which he can structure the response the idea requires.

Unfortunately, at the same time the brain's performance seems miraculous, our history and our environment demonstrate that when its attributes are directed toward wrong goals (disharmony), its accomplishments are delivered at the terrible expense of a cumulative pollution of the world with the debris of man's selfishness. His goals have remained horizontally disposed and feature his circumspect, lifetime, earthbound formula for satisfaction—his personal satisfaction. He has failed to sense the significance of the staging of the earthbound event for the vertical launching of his consciousness on an eternal course. The dust he leaves behind may very well be molded again and again into an earthly form that can hold his spirit until the real message of his life is perceived.

In the animal world we see Will simply as 'the will to live', but in man's case we see this 'will to live' take on another dimension that reveals his innate sense of something special about himself (which he may or may not recognize). In man we see the 'will to live' extended to the 'will to live forever' (consciously or not). Even in the earthbound mechanical setting we notice man continually trying to extend his life cycle through the dispensations of his physician; and virtually everyone has some ceremonial prayer offered for his 'eternal soul' when his breathing stops. Man is disenchanted with the idea of life ending even though he may have given it little attention during his toyfilled existence. Somewhere in the subterranean layers of his mind he dreams of 'living forever'. Something in him whispers that somewhere (heaven?), under some other circumstance, he will be understood and rewarded with eternal life.

What we notice is that the mobilization of Will in behalf of an eternal goal varies in intensity within the human family. To draw attention to the dynamics of it we could think of it as wattage. Wattage is power (energy). Two electric light bulbs may look alike in size and shape but when they are plugged in they may yield quite different quantities of light. Men too differ in the amount of illumination they deliver when plugged into the circuitry of certain higher ideas. The wattage of their 'Wills' to execute an action in behalf of higher goals is considerably different based in all probability on the degree of motion that has already been made in behalf of a search for the answer to the inner question—Who Am I? But, unlike the light bulb that must live out its 'wattage time' as it is stamped, man can increase his Will as he exercises it in behalf of his goal. Will can grow with use. With no use, or, with abortive attention to a goal, Will can fade to a flicker. It is through this mysterious alchemy that the brain's electrical pattern can be energized to a finer, higher level of electrical performance—a level that will permit the opening up of new circuits, bypassing the old, ancient, habitual, survival-reproductive pathways of lower forms (and mechanical man) except for certain obvious needs consistent with our protoplasmic heritage.

If man accepts the challenge of the search, if the wish and the Will are sufficient to proceed, the first step toward a higher goal consists in making an assay of the equipment—the space suit and its vital systems.

Man has forgotten his body was prepared for the earthly sojourn of the creative spirit that seeks expression through his actions under the supervision of his brain which is prepared to direct the ensemble of body cells to function in concert toward homeostasis. The brain during this earthly mission called 'life' is charged as in lower forms with the responsibility for the body's proper maintenance and use. It knows the need of every cell by virtue of the gathered proven knowledge of instinct which has been purged of serious error through eons of survival performance. It is man's cerebral override in behalf of his appetites that has interfered with the integrity of the message of instinct, the appropriate programmer of the body's function. His value system, warped by his laziness and distorted by his social view of the meaning of work, has allowed the body to call for its pleasures through his most sophisticated instrumentation—the cerebral cortex. Through its own demands, the body has penetrated and usurped the function of this miraculous computer, designed for spectacular innovation in behavioral response, for the comparatively meager, trite tasks of eating and reproducing. It is instinct that is prepared and stands ready (when permitted) to preserve the integrity of the body's life cycle and thereby release man's higher circuitry for higher goals.

It would help man in his health efforts to see disease of the body as evidence of his own misuse of the brain, which, when properly activated, can bring his tissues into the harmony intended for them. Health under these arrangements becomes the consequence of the harmony within the body as the brain accepts its proper charge to function as the instrument of an expanding consciousness.

To assess the equipment—our bodies—and engage in a program of purification and health goals (a return to homeostasis) is just a beginning, however. We must then turn our attention to an observation of ourselves as behavioral manifestations of a force within us. We must watch ourselves move and function from a detached position in an entirely new way which seems at first as though we were noticing someone else. We must see what kind of mechanical, automatic, habit-formed patterns of reaction have been established in our toy negotiations.

It will probably be disturbing to see how predictable our actions have been. We may even resist the idea that we have not been spontaneous and creative, but continued observation will destroy this notion. Although we may think we have been making fresh decisions, we will find they have been stereotyped, almost fixed decisions, established as appropriate for us in the marketplace as we fall into the mechanical type of our Essence—physical, intellectual, or emotional. We will see we are truly creatures of habit, programmed with negativity, and as ordinary mechanical man, we are set on automatic for destruction.

By watching closely, we will see how we costume up for each occasion in the marketplace. We will discover the nature of the wardrobe we have chosen for ourselves for movement through the herd. We will be able to see how we have structured Personality to cover up Essence (our true feelings) in behalf of toy business. But also, we will see rare glimpses of Essence at times when Personality fails as the negotiator and Essence breaks through the mask, for no costume is perfect. But the inadvertent disclosure of Essence, perhaps in the midst of a tedious transaction, if we are aware, can be instrumental in our beginning to see ourselves, if we are observing ourselves. True knowledge begins with self-observation.

To rediscover Essence, it is helpful to examine our childhood where it performed before Personality covered it up. Relatives and friends can sometimes help to fill in gaps where recall refuses to go. When the events of childhood have been too traumatic to permit recollection, hypnosis has been strategically used to bring buried facts into view. Also, sometimes we will see Essence tear off the costume in moments of emotional extremes. Rage, grief, and ecstasy can disarm and decostume us sufficiently at times that we can see our basic formula—our true nature. Though not recommended, alcohol or certain drugs will destroy our organization sufficiently to cause us to drop the masquerade, leaving us exposed as we really are. Whatever the technique, it is important to see what kind of Essence it was that required the kind of costumes we fashioned to hide it. To understand ourselves and our behavioral manifestation we must let fall the costume of Personality and be willing to face what we see. Usually, when we see ourselves, one way or another, we also see where the work needs to be done, for the spirit has chosen the atmosphere of earth to find its path back to its source through the revelations disclosed to us through our behavior. As we live our lives more and more consciously, it works toward the harmony conceived in its creation. It is free choice, Will, that permitted us to wander off the path and it is free choice, Will, that must realign us with the spirit's Providential goal. The spirit is perfect because it was created with the first breath of Providence, a perfect Entity. It is the manifestation that is imperfect and has produced the disharmony we currently feel. The disparity between the spirit and the manifestation produces suffering and shows us what kind of work needs to be done not only for mankind, but for each constituent in the human experiment, for we are all connected by the same breath of Providence.

Work directed toward narrowing this gap between the spirit and the manifestation brings a new dimension to the suffering we spoke of earlier when considering ordinary mechanical man. At that time, the sufferings happened to us, since they were the consequence of the difference between things as we thought they were and things as they really were. But upon awakening to this reality even partially we must include also a kind of suffering that is the consequence of the difference between things as they really are and things as they ought to be as we begin to sense what is needed for our own completion. This second phase of suffering comes to replace mechanical suffering (which contributes little or nothing to our growth). We could call it intentional suffering for it is the result of a conscious effort to begin to work and to do what is essential for our own fulfillment.

To *be*. We must see ourselves as we are. We must see both the wardrobe and what it hides. When we see ourselves we will no doubt experience a sense of incompleteness. This feeling of only *being in part* precipitates a wish *to become*—to become complete in our manifestation on earth—and this establishes our new goal. *To become* we must work toward the fulfillment of the idea we represent—the spiritual formula that seeks manifestation through us. The work required by this translation of the idea to its complete manifestation we can call *doing*.

Before we can *do*, we must first *see ourselves* at the beginning of the path toward our new goal. At the same time, we must utilize the brain's faculty for symbolism to catch glimpses of the structure and feeling content we see as a harmonious possibility for ourselves through the energy that the idea we hold provides. Through an inner visualization, fostered by the advancing accuracy of our creative imaginations in behalf of a high goal, we must sense the nature of the behavioral implications required to move in the direction of it. Through a combination of prayerful supplication to acknowledged higher forces, through meditation, and serious contemplation by becoming very quiet within, we must let the idea circulate, using the brain's organization to project its social future. In this way we can choose, as a temporary experiment, what seems to be ideal for us based on what we have already discovered through self-observation. We cannot know from the start what is precisely ideal for us because experiencing is part of knowing, but we can paint a picture that continues to gather new brushmarks as we assemble the data from the by-products of our new performance, altering the motion we make as we proceed on a path toward inner and outer harmony. As we grow in conscious recognition of our own inner state, we will simultaneously sharpen our ability to foresee what is best for us.

It is timely to note that all ideas already exist. With the 'big bang' the physicists speak of, Providence created all things. Some ideas we do not yet see on a physical basis, not only because our vision is limited, but also because the conditions necessary for certain manifestations are still being prepared. To say it another way—the 'big bang' is still banging or, in more graceful terms, the initial creative pulse wave is still surging. The manifestation must await the proper setting. Every idea has its requirements for full delivery. In the case of man, in both the overview and the short view, we see the idea only in part. We must fill the gap, for the present, with the skills of our creative imaginations which extend man's present recognition of his dimensions and permit him to move with the creative process. Man is still being created. Through his Will he has the opportunity to finish his creation, but he must choose to do so. He has been set free in the universe with the task of translating the idea he represents to the harmonious behavioral form the idea declares. It is man who can give the idea expression through his actions.

We should remember the idea carries with it the potential energy required to give it expression. The higher the idea, the greater the energy incorporated in it. The impulse is always from the idea to its manifestation. The spirit *wishes* to be made flesh. Ideas are in a sense electrical dynamos and they are launched at the time of creation fully capable of their own fulfillment in proper season. They have specific structural features which carry a vibrational signal that the brain is prepared to receive if properly attuned. They are too finely structured for our coarse sensory organization to define them as such. Nonetheless, they have dimensions and through the resources of their energy allotments they stand ready to affect the universe, in accordance with their force and direction, gaining in their influence as they move toward their manifestation.

If we receive an idea of profound consequence such as the idea to truly manifest 'love', the possibility for an act of love to ensue exists though it is not guaranteed. Through the brain's mysterious organization we can translate the fine vibrations of so rich an aim into a sensory demonstration of it, a behavioral enactment of it. The challenge does not rest with the idea, for the idea is perfect and ready. The challenge rests with us who are to manifest it. The quality of the manifestation depends upon the quality of our perception of it and the magnitude of our Will to act upon it fully. Our concerns need not center on the validity of the idea 'to love', but rather they should center on the validity of our response to it. This falls short because of the limitations we may have unwisely imposed on its full expression through previous entrenched commitments to the survival dialogue. To change under these circumstances requires exceptional courage.

If we remember the process through which we learned to walk, discovering through repeated error the law of gravity, we may get a concept of what may be required to learn a much more complex act—to love. We learned the law of gravity because, first, we harbored the wish to walk. Repeated failures during the earlier years, though painful at times, did not alter the goal. Through practice, the will to walk raised the quality of the performance to improved levels. The brain was commandeered by the challenge to record the physics of the action and redefine the reaction, gradually gathering the information necessary for the refinement in the interpretation of the stimuli offered by the law of gravity. Through these accrued experiences consisting of successes and failures in execution, a full understanding of the law was reached and perfect balance and harmonious movement resulted. For some, it did not end here. The grace of the human form in movement was set to music and beautiful behavioral expression of the law of gravity was made manifest as an art form in dance and ballet. From the crudest waddle to the pirouette was an extension of the behavioral wish to walk. It began with the wish and was completed by the combination of will, suffering, work, the experiencing of successes and failures, and finally an understanding. For some it became also the wise and beautiful act of sharing a graceful rendition for the enjoyment and betterment of others.

The recipe for any understanding of life—physical or metaphysical—is essentially the same. Persistent motion in the direction of the goal is required. Knowledge (book learning) without action can never be experience, and understanding without experience is impossible.

The bruises of physical learning are somewhat obvious. The bruises of metaphysical learning may be slower and more subtle in their appearance though they need not be. If we are trying to learn to love for instance, our failures can be hidden from view for a time, but eventually they do rise to the surface and disclose the nature of our performance. Intended love frequently veers from its course and takes a turn backwards to love of self-image—to selfishness. The bruise we suffer as a result of selfish action may be slow in revealing itself, but the law that has been violated, like the law of gravity, is sufficiently specific and precise, that the bruise will for certain show itself (the Law of Compensation; we reap what we sow). Sometimes an act performed in ignorance will promote the same sequence. Ignorance does not provide us with protection from penalties of violating the law any more than ignorance of the law of gravity protected us from falling as we learned to walk in those early days.

In order to process the wish 'to love' through the brain's circuitry, it must first be properly prepared for so complex, so powerful, and yet so delicate a transmission. We cannot just wake up one day and decide 'to love' everyone. It is a learned art just as walking is a learned art. Most of life's events are a part of the preparation for this greatest act if man is to be complete and to move harmoniously. The 'school of hard knocks,' which rather tersely conveys the abrasive nature of day to day living (no matter who you are), is life beating us into a kind of submission if we awaken to ourselves. We must be in a proper inner state if we are *to love*.

If the hand touches a hot stove, the impulse traveling to the brain is processed quickly and produces a withdrawal of the hand in a split second. The action is so fast we have given it a word—reflex. Only afterwards does the brain raise the experience to a cerebral level, consider the information further, and perhaps call upon other responses if the event is serious enough.

Ideas are also a form of stimulation though the circuitry required to manifest them is much more complex. The electrical path through the brain is much more obscure and difficult to trace because it not only may take years for the idea to materialize, it may take lifetimes.

To gather an impression of the complexity of the brain itself, let alone the complexity of the idea it is given to process, consider that the cerebral cortex alone is made up of over fifty billion nerve cells. Each of these nerve cells has probably ten thousand axonal and dendritic connections. And each chromosome of every cell is capable of handling millions of 'bits' of information. Add to this the feature that each connection has thousands of terminal plates where augmentation, inhibition, or even cancellation of the impulse can occur. To this add that every cell resonates at all times with the electrical vibration that identifies the individual in the universe just as your signature identifies you. If this were not enough, think of yourself as being part of an electrical universe in which everything is connected through electromagnetic force fields by a superluminal process that makes the knowledge of all events simultaneous and instantaneous. What we are saying is that the brain presents as many electrical opportunities as there are sands in the sea and stars in the sky and more. Our minds, so conditioned to ordinary sequential matters have trouble handling the magnitude of such a concept.

If the brain seizes upon just one idea such as the wish 'to love', it is equipped sufficiently to carry that idea eventually to its fruition, but to handle such a charge, its circuitry must be made ready to receive and process it. It cannot be already overloaded with the noise of local survival dialogue. It cannot be cluttered and preoccupied with extraneous, earthbound, nuisance information. The wish to receive must be evident to alter the brain's circuitry. The wish becomes the prayer for greater understanding. If the wish is there, some form of meditation can assist us in placing the brain in a proper receptive state. When sitting quietly with eyes closed, perhaps performing an inner exercise of disengagement, the brain can be subtly placed in a state of special receptivity sufficiently sensitive to tune in to the fine, high vibrations that surround its electrical force field. Though the vibrations are fine, they carry a high electrical charge of energy.

When the idea first reaches the brain's circuitry, it is not in language form—it is not literary—but exists only with its own vibrational electrical signature. It becomes the brain's chore to conduct this idea through its relay systems in such a way that the idea can be given symbolism through words which suggest the nature of its intellectual and emotional content. Only by beginning with the brain's symbols can the idea find its way into actualization on the experiential side.

While this cannot be done without our collaboration, we must be quick to notice we are not authors of the idea—we are the transmitters of it—and as such we have no right to pride. If we deliver the message of the idea harmoniously, we can only be thankful for the opportunity to have become an instrument for sounding it.

The first motion on the side of actualization of the idea requires something special. The first step in delivering the message requires faith. Faith fills the interval between contemplation and actualization. With the motion of the idea on the experiential side, we are subject to local judgment and a lingering agony over the censorship of our peers. The first step is a critical step for it commits us to the idea. Not until we act upon it have we revealed our sense of it. Faith with action becomes a belief system. Faith is then replaced by understanding as we experience the result action has produced. If the idea belongs to the Providential scheme, further steps will gather support derived from the product of the previous ones and the action becomes justified by the outcome. Added to the understanding arising from the experiences the idea has heralded is the ultimate gift of Providence to crown the sequence—wisdom. Wisdom is the ability to use the understanding one has acquired to promote harmonious goals in the human experiment—ultimately, universal harmony—oneness with God, one's neighbor, and one's self. This examination of the translation of the idea 'to love' to its highest form of enactment through the complex circuitry of the human brain we could well call 'the anatomy of a miracle'.

This chain of events is an electrical transaction of consciousness every bit as discernable and definable as the more self-evident example of withdrawing the hand from a hot stove. It simply requires more circuitry. Loosely we call the complete cycle thinking, feeling and doing. The pain-remedy sequence of the hot stove example belongs to instinct—to the survival theme that has been rehearsed through time. The idea-manifestation sequence, however, is relatively new. It belongs to man. With his special endowment, he can absorb the content of the idea 'to love', and with innovation and creativity, alloted to his equipment, he can ultimately express it.

Through self-observation and self-remembering, there is a continuing awareness of the structure and deployment of Essence and Personality. They are both more and more completely exposed. Sometimes the revelations are of such a nature that a feeling of despair reaches us, especially at the beginning when one day we suddenly see the false nature of the marketplace and of our own false selves. We might even entertain an impulse to throw the whole wardrobe away as a kind of cleansing denial of the very idea of negotiating through a false self. But to take such a step would point us in the wrong direction albeit for the right reason. Even if the costumes of Personality could momentarily be 'ripped off' through defiance and disgust, would not our Essence suffer premature exposure and incapacity to perform directly? Essence does not arrive as a perfect messenger of Providence, for it comes to earth with a need that life here provides for its own completion. If such a hypothetical act of defiance did in fact take place, it would in all probability be in the absence of any prior work on Essence during its lifetime. The impulse to destroy the costumes that offer protection in a scene of hypocrisy must be replaced by a work toward a rightly balanced relationship of these two fundamental components of human nature.

Before Essence can benefit from its experience on earth, before it can grow or evolve, we must learn to observe the real structure of our human nature (physical, intellectual and emotional). To discover this helps us to discover also what needs to be done to bring balance to this combination of body, mind, and feelings. At moments, when these elements can be brought to function in harmony toward the same goal, real motion is possible. During this time of assessment the marketplace provides us with the mirror that will help us see ourselves and any changes we may be making. Our value system, having changed as a part of a new direction, will cause us to function differently even though we use the same old costumes.

One may preserve the costumes of Personality and continue to transact toy business while discovery and learning continue. What man notices is that gradually he will be wearing his costumes more and more consciously. He will be 'in costume' when necessary and 'out of costume' when opportune. As a result he will come to be more in harmony with his universe as he gains in knowledge, experience, understanding, and wisdom.

Inner growth in no way asks us to abort the obligations of

outer growth, our responsibility for the physical form—the space suit and its appendages. It only places our attention on them in the subordinate role they deserve. As long as we have protoplasm, we will have physical commitments to fulfill, and we will need to go to the marketplace to pay suitable homage to the needs of the body. Regardless of our inner aim, we are still faced during our life cycle with the challenges of survival, reproduction and physical pleasure, though they are no longer our major goals. Our attention on them becomes limited though not forgotten. What we notice is that by shifting our aim toward a higher target there will develop a change in attitude about the marketplace and about toy business. We may laugh at what we see and do, as our insight improves. Mostly we will notice our toy negotiations will be conducted so that no harm comes to anyone as a result of them. A strange paradox follows. This feeling of detachment, this ability not to identify with our costumes or the toys that pass through our hands unexpectedly increases the effectiveness of our performance. To our surprise toys tend to flow toward us. In fact any toy a man needs is there to be had as long as the appreciation of it is in harmony with his development. As our relationship to the marketplace changes, we will notice we will be more and more able to penetrate the masquerades and energy will not be wasted.

In the marketplace we will notice our progress from time to time as we see a change in our behavior when certain issues repeat themselves. Since the pattern of life is cyclic, the issues that face us tend to recur. Instead of traveling in a tight circle, repeating our mistakes as ordinary mechanical man, we may find our new path as Transitional Man is that of an expanding spiral. When we meet the same challenge as before, we may see we have elevated our perspective and broadened our response to the issue because our consciousness has been raised, and our sense of reality has expanded.

To a man on one slope of a mountain it can be a sunny day. To a man on the opposite side it may be a rainy day. To a man on the summit it can be both a sunny and rainy day. Such is reality—such is truth.

But how does man learn about truth? How can he begin on his new path and be sure he is moving in the right direction? We said earlier, to transact toy business more successfully, we needed education (earthbound knowledge) that had bargaining value. Choosing a school for this purpose was relatively simple for the curriculum was more or less standardized for the task chosen. We also need instruction to move toward the goal of higher consciousness. It is especially important for such an aim that our learning be attended to expertly, for we are dealing with elusive issues and the way is more hidden. Choosing a teacher in this realm is much more difficult, for we are entering into new dimensions beyond the measuring devices of the sensory world. Many charlatans and false prophets fill the gap between spiritual awakening and spiritual fulfillment. But there are certain clues to the wise teacher. We will notice that the dialogue of the true teacher is matched by the action. It is what the teacher produces that reveals the reality of the teaching. ("By their fruits you shall know them.") A new value scale should open up to us and a judgment can be made as we see the results of our own action through behavioral change.

We will notice also as communication with a higher force continues, to be in the presence of a true teacher releases a kind of energy that compounds the enthusiasm for higher goals. Remembering that energy is substance, we can observe that in a real exchange between teacher and pupil (seeker), we gather a new force—a special energy that accentuates the wish and the Will 'to be' and 'to do'.

The laws we need to learn under this new circumstance, though simple, are more difficult to accept because they are simple, and because they run counter to what we have more than likely been taught in most instances in survival instruction. It is also very important to notice that the lessons for each individual will be different, at least in sequence, and especially at the beginning, for we each have our own Essence to deal with. We are each starting with a different beginning organization, and accordingly different needs. The question 'Who Am I?' is brought to consciousness under specific circumstances for each individual. It is because of this specific difference in the challenges each person must meet that standardized teaching and formal generalizations are dangerous, if not impossible. The same classroom techniques useful for toy business cannot be applied except as a forum for the practice of what we are learning in a group, fused by common wishes for higher knowledge. The same advice cannot be given each person, and the sage's voice may speak differently to each individual at the start. This feature is sometimes misunderstood, and may even give the appearance of contradiction if we were to compare the prescriptions dispensed to us, but actually the phenomenon only demonstrates the specific difference in the need of each person at the commencement of his 'doing'.

Usually 'doing' commences with 'undoing', for our computers, our brains, have been programmed with negativity by the social order which uses fear as the vehicle for its message of neat, sleepy conformity. Through this device we have solidified our type-established habitual performance—and the circuitry of negation has become the easy electrical route through the brain. The circuits have become jammed with endless 'don'ts' and few 'do's'. Usually even the 'do's' are a backlash of the 'don'ts'—of negation. We hear little of the goodness of the spirit of man and the natural beauty it can bring spontaneously to his actions within the framework of universal harmony. We wind up trying to 'live right' for the wrong reason.

If our true goal is to seek the true, complete manifestation of ourselves, the native joy in completing the idea is the only discipline we need, for such a path is in harmony with Providential design. Under this circumstance, the 'don'ts' would fall away leaving the manifestation, already within universal law, with its own beauty. Under this propellant we 'do right' because of what harmonious action produces. 'Right doing', as the result of right motive, moves under its own force. We no longer 'do right' out of fear of 'doing wrong' or to gain a material reward (selfishness), but because 'right doing' brings harmony within and without. With such action the law of balance at a higher dimension is learned. When man's actions bring disharmony to him, he is falling away from the target he has chosen. He must try again and again.

Through his awakening, his spiritual birth, man falls heir to an act of Providential grace. The forces of higher consciousness are open to him. By virtue of his choice to move in a new direction, he falls under the jurisdiction of Providential Law, and proceeds with a new understanding of the unrelenting influence of Cosmological Law (Natural Law), and escapes untimely intrusions of the Law of Accident.

Because each of us is an individual with specificity and uniqueness, our sense of God, our sense of the creative force we are prone to watch, will also be unique at the start since we each perceive this force from a slightly different angle. For this reason we each in a sense become our own religion. Under this provision there will be as many religions as there are people on earth. We each have our own need, our own earthly task, our own prayer, our own creed, our own offering, our own atonement, and our own thanksgiving. As we draw closer to our goal—our sense of completeness—we will not only see ourselves better, but we will see our neighbor and our God better also. For in our attainment of knowledge, understanding, and wisdom, we will be moving with more grace toward the pinnacle where all religions merge into one because God, Neighbor, and Self are One.

We can gain a visual image of what the project is about if we picture a mountain with people starting at various points on a climb to the top. The circumstances of each climb will be different because each person is different. Some will start out on the north side and the condition there will be different than on the south, or the east, or the west by reason of external forces. Our paths will be such that eventually we will come to know and understand all of these forces in our own climb for nothing is left out if we are to be complete. Some, because of their natures (their Essence), will begin to ascend from the rocky side, others will seek the forest, some the rivers, and still others the desert; but the pathway we must take eventually winds through all of them, for by Providential design man is commissioned to gain total experience so that nothing is missed. Some travelers will have a great Will, possibly seasoned by previous attempts to climb the mountain and, remembering the lessons of previous lifetimes, they may move more swiftly toward the top. Others may wander for years having no direction, losing sight of the goal, descending many times when climbing would have been better. Some fall by the wayside, forgetting the whole project. Others may wander from place to place for years, trying this and that, looking for short cuts. Others become overwhelmed and may become too ill to continue. As we climb higher, we will notice the number of pilgrims has thinned out but we will also notice they are closer together because mastery of climbing brings them closer together in thought, word, and deed. Though at the beginning there were many pathways, as we come higher, they begin to merge, for as man moves upward, he comes closer to a sense of the singleness, of completeness and harmony—universal harmony.

Perhaps we will be better able to grasp the nature of Transitional Man's project if we examine a single trait and follow its course through the possible sequence of changes we have been describing. Suppose that as a part of his Essence he was born with a very fearful nature. His self-observation of his behavioral program might reveal him to be a person of the emotional type. From his reactions to various stimuli he might describe his basic animal nature (his Essence) as that of a deer. To survive he 'runs and hides'. He notices he is constantly on the lookout for danger, for since he is not equipped for violence, his life depends on his alertness and his sharp sensitive perception of his surroundings. He is ready to run at the slightest provocation from both real and imaginary threats. To be a prisoner of this fear produces a certain kind of suffering. At the marketplace, where 'the jungle' meets, toy bargaining is going to be painful, for the theme is *violence*. There he will be easily injured, maybe even sacrificed, if he attempts to negotiate toy deals through his fearful *Essence*. More than likely he will choose not to go to the marketplace any more often than is absolutely necessary and his tendency will be to shy away from people.

Still there are some items he must obtain from the marketplace, and he discovers he can acquire certain toys by costuming up, by exploiting other aspects of his emotional nature. Very cleverly at times he may be able to achieve a toy goal by 'putting on an act', by pretending, by fashioning an image, structuring his Personality in such a way that he can hide his fear and at the same time fill his needs and desires in the midst of the social order. Through practice in costuming he can at least fill his survival and procreation demands. But this operation *per se* is a cover-up only, and he remains an ordinary mechanical man (in this case an emotional type), a prisoner of fear, for his inner basic reaction is still 'to run and hide', and because of this his suffering continues though it is buried. His acts have become repetitious and actually he runs in a very tight predictable circle, sometimes running from the very experience he needs in order to grow, to complete his destiny.

In the midst of this circumstance, one day the questions reach him—Who am I? What am I running from? These questions can be the beginning of change. As his observation continues with these questions in mind, he will notice that most of the time he is running from experiences that in retrospect held no real danger. His fear was imaginary. Through memory, coupled to his self-awareness, he becomes able to see that fear is not an appropriate response for most events, and that actually he misses something by running away. At this point a teacher can be of help to him. The teacher, through creating the situation whereby he can see himself better, can instruct him through his own doing not only about the marketplace but about himself as well. Fear finds a new place in his value scale. Reading about fear, studying books about overcoming fear will not be enough because understanding requires experience and this means exposure through 'doing'. He cannot simply say, for instance, "I will control my fear," for the more he tries to control it with his mind, the more imbedded the fear reaction becomes. Instead of controlling fear he must first fully sense it and then preempt it. He must place before himself the possibility of alternative reactions that subsequent experience verifies are more fulfilling. He does not want to abandon fear, because in a world of violence it would be foolish to give up the protection that a sensitive nature offers. He does want to defuse fear and allow other dimensions of behavioral response to contribute to the marketplace manifestation. He wants to change the program that certain stimuli provoke and through experience, supervised by a teacher who already has understanding, he will conclude that running away from an experience cannot be allowed to become the automatic answer, for he will be also running away from what he needs in order to grow. Subsequently, instead of suffering the automatic consequence of the fear dilemma (as ordinary mechanical man), he turns this suffering by his attention to it into conscious suffering. That is, he deliberately accepts it and explores all of the consequences of other alternatives, examining fear through his experience until it takes a subordinate position that permits motion. In this case he becomes a Transitional Man. He grows and develops as he raises his consciousness in behalf of his goal.

Sooner or later he may discover he has grown antlers. This revelation can become an exciting part of his growth and development. Instead of running he may choose to lower them on some occasions and stand his ground, not only in the interest of his own development, but for the benefit of everyone. For whenever man escapes his mechanical animal bondage, all mankind benefits. Every step that is made toward one's inner goal is a precious step if one remembers the alternative is emptiness.

The illustration we have chosen to think about regarding fear is useful to emphasize the fact that the sage cannot offer the same advice to every traveler. Whereas in the case of the man whose Essence resembled that of the deer discovering his antlers might have been an exciting step in his growth and development, suppose by contrast his Essence were that of a bull. Under this circumstance, to call attention to the power and virtue of horns would be ridiculous, maybe even tragic. His project will take an entirely different course and his task may be to forget his horns—at least for a time. The wisdom of a guide must be relied upon through the labyrinth to self-discovery until one's own knowledge becomes substantiated by experience, understanding, and hopefully wisdom.

One more analogy may help us to grasp the complexity of man's challenge and yet perhaps provide us with a sense of what is possible.

Suppose we think of creation as a great symphonic master-piece composed in every detail by God, Himself. Now without someone to attempt a rendition of this composition not much would come of it, for it is only when the sounds fashioned in the composer's mind are instrumented that the measure of its beauty can be appreciated. Thus, as part of the orchestration of creation, man was fashioned in God's image so that His omnipresent, omnipotent and omniscient self could listen to the sounds of His own score. Each man is an orchestra and is given the task to learn the music and play it for the glorification of God. Now at the time each man awakens to this opportunity and sense of his real meaning, he finds on examining himself and looking at his orchestra that very much work needs to be done. First of all, he finds he has been playing a great deal with just the brass and the percussion section because he likes noise and volume. The violinists can hardly be heard and with eyes closed they are off in another world playing very high notes. The wind section with their flutes and oboes are only salivating, getting ready—always getting ready. The harpist is crouched in the wings with her fingers in her ears. The pianist is only three, cannot reach the hold pedal, and insists he would rather play the cymbals anyway.

There are limitless excursions into a world of confusion we could continue with to describe this orchestra, let alone the conductor (ourself), who has just seen the music for the first time. (When he passed it out, each member of the orchestra was certain his piece was a solo part.)

It is easy to see that the infinite number of steps that must be taken to bring order out of this chaos is out of the reach of language, for in all of this dialogue about man, words give us only hints of what we really mean anyway. We must depend on each other to round out the inner meaning behind each syllable, but when we look at the stars we can sense beyond our vocabularies that order can be brought out of chaos, and that we are a part of that task.

To bring order to our orchestra, the conductor needs to understand every measure of the composition. He must then command the attention of every member of his ensemble, adding new instruments in the weaker sections, and restraining others until they all hear the beauty of harmony and respect his authority in directing a rendition of it. With much work, much suffering, much practice through the noise and struggles of error, the sounds of creation begin to come through. Finally, with learned grace and love, the Self, the Master I, beckons skillfully to his complement of violins when delicate threads of the theme are needed, and calls with deliberate sweeps of his arms for the crash of cymbals when emphasis offers refinement to the music. The pianist plays his interludes beautifully, having grown up and become able to reach the pedal. The whole orchestra now plays in balance and the violinist has learned to love the drummer. The music of this harmonious state has brought the full spectrum of the sounds of creation to consciousness and declares with its message we are all separately one.

How can we summarize the subject of Transitional Man? There is danger in attempting any simplistic recipe for living, but there are certain key words that are useful to keep the task alive. The steps begin with the arrival of a question— Who Am I? If man harbors a wish to respond to such a question with all of the upheavals associated with the revelation of the answer, he must generate the Will required to take him through the many successes and failures he undoubtedly will experience. He needs to begin with self-observation in an effort to see not only his Essence but also his Personality, which he structured for his own protection in the marketplace. He must examine the motive behind each of his actions, and sense the reality in every experience. To reach his lifetime goal for universal harmony, he must establish short range goals in keeping with the preparation necessary for him to process finer vibrations through his instrument of consciousness, his brain. He must commit himself to the idea by 'doing', by acting upon the idea, gaining thereby an understanding of harmony. He will need to seek help through a teacher who has preceded him on the way. He must remember himself if he is to change. He must move with a sense of thanksgiving for the opportunity life affords him to see himself and to help others to see also. Finally, he must walk in the harmony he discovers with compassion, the highest note in the octave of love, for this is the glorification of God.

A man who proceeds on such a path will discover with a growing realization that God, his Neighbor and Himself are One.

CHAPTER VII

A FANTASY OF MAN

WHEN WE HAVE LIBERATED the human brain from its entrapment in the physical world, we can turn it loose in the realm of ideas, remembering that what we imagine to be possible is possible. What fantasy does our view of creation describe for man? What kind of a world do we dream of? And why do we think of it as tomorrow's world?

We sometimes tire ourselves and lose sight of our goals because we think of them as being so far away, but time is our illusion, it is not Providence's illusion. It is we who are in the time-space dimension. If God is omniscient, omnipotent, and omnipresent, He is certainly not located in either time or space. Sometimes we get stuck on words like tomorrow, yesterday, time, and space, in terms of our own goals. We tend to look at the present as fixed and our dreams as far away in the future, already marred by our past. Our programming, once again based on fear, has taught us to feel guilty about our failures and to worry about our future. The past, we say, is over with and cannot be changed. It is difficult to grasp even a fleeting glimpse of the idea of timelessness and spacelessness intellectually, yet we can single out experiences of special consciousness and insight that brought us the feeling that time had stopped—that we were a part of forever, yet nowhere in particular. At some point we must startle ourselves with the realization that everything that was and will be, already is. Our dreams stand waiting for us now.

Through symbols we can sometimes see things more clearly. We can resolve some of the confusion surrounding time and space by thinking of ourselves looking at a spot on the ground. We can say we are looking at this particular spot at this particular time. Now we move a few yards away and look at another spot at a different point in time. Looking at these two spots in sequence represents our level of perspective at the time of the experiment. We can say our consciousness was very close to earth. Now suppose we climb a ladder and look down from a somewhat higher position. We find then we can see both spots at once. From this height we are looking at an area 'now' which formerly we saw as 'past and future'. By a change in perspective, an increase in consciousness, we have erased the sense of time and space for the two spots.

Suppose we climb in our consciousness *ad infinitum*. We will then see everything with a new sense of vision and all will be 'now'. With this expansion in consciousness, past, present, and future become one, and the whole universe becomes a single happening.

But the universe, even in the 'now', is dynamic. It does not sit motionless. It vibrates in varying wavelengths from the smallest subatomic particle to the largest galaxy. While there is plus, there is simultaneously minus. Action is always met by reaction, but in this arena of polarity the opposing forces are not precisely equal. There is always enough imbalance either on the plus side or the minus side for change to occur— motion. If the forces were exactly equal, they would cancel each other out and there would be a stalemate—immobility— no change. Still, as a witness, we see either chaotic order or ordered chaos in both the microcosm and macrocosm. The overall result of our observations reveals the presence of a total plan within these worlds of imbalanced polarities. It is not a world of haphazard collision. There is some reconciling force that steers this imbalance. The motions are noted to occur with sufficient regularity to allow us to observe certain universal laws (such as the law of gravity). Since there is an overall orderliness in this universe composed of worlds of positive-negative imbalance, there must be a special force (Primal Force, Creative Force, Providence, God) that not only placed the whole cosmos in motion—a force that brings order to chaos—but a force that knows also what direction each particle and galaxy must take to fulfill itself as part of creation. Such a force knows the destiny of all motion, all change, *now*.

It is this creative force that monitors the balance between plus and minus. It is this force we speak of as God that knows and understands every human being and his potential fulfillment. It is this force that understands galaxies and at the same time notices the fall of a sparrow, because everything in the universe is connected. It is this reconciling force that becomes the lingering memory of Providence and monitors creation. It is this same sense of a Providential force that gives us permission to move creatively, and to implement what we imagine as the full potential of man 'now'. The plan is there. It is up to us to discover it and to manifest it.

In the mind of every Man there rests an illusion—
An illusion called 'tomorrow'.
'Tomorrow' is that distant land
We would fill with what is missing from today.
And what is it we would put off
And crowd into a future moment

When we have this one—
A now that never stops.

To have this moment perfect
We must be willing to give away yesterday and tomorrow
For there is no past or future
As far as the heart is concerned.
It knows only its perpetual need
For perfect blending and harmony.
It wishes for nothing else
Than to love and be loved—NOW!

from *Golden Threads*
by Mark Coventry
(pen name of Franklin Earnest III)